ADDICTED TO MEDIOCRITY

BY FRANKY SCHAEFFER V

Principal One-man Shows—Painting

Frisch Gallery, New York, N.Y. (March 1970)
Garden Center, Tulsa, Okla. (February 1971)
Criteria Arts, London, U.K. (November 1972)
Galerie Chante-Pierre, Aubonne, Switzerland (1974-75)

Films

Created/produced *How Should We Then Live?*
(5 hours, 16 mm. color) 1974-75
Screenplay by and directed *Whatever Happened to the Human Race?*
(5 hours, 16 mm. color) 1977-79
Directed/hosted *Reclaiming the World*
(5 hours, 16 mm. color) 1981
Directed *The Second American Revolution*
(30 minutes, 35 mm. color) 1981-82
Produced *The Great Evangelical Disaster*
(30 minutes, 16 mm. color) 1984

Books

Coauthor of *Plan for Action* (Revell 1979-80)
Addicted to Mediocrity (Crossway Books 1981)
A Time for Anger (Crossway Books 1982)
Bad News for Modern Man (Crossway Books 1984)
A Modest Proposal, with Harold Fickett (Thomas Nelson 1985)

Newspaper

The Christian Activist, editor

ADDICTED
TO
MEDIOCRITY

20th Century Christians and the Arts

—*Revised edition*—

FRANKY
SCHAEFFER

Illustrations by Kurt Mitchell

CROSSWAY BOOKS • WHEATON, ILLINOIS
A DIVISION OF GOOD NEWS PUBLISHERS

14 13 12 11 10 09 08 07 06 05
19   18   17   16   15   14   13   12   11   10

To Genie, my wife, whom I love and like.
Her life is a work of art in itself, her
friendship peace in a troubled world.

CONTENTS

ACKNOWLEDGMENTS

First I would like to thank my wife, Genie, and my three children, Francis, Jessica, and John, for providing a home and an environment that is conducive to creativity, love and beauty. Without them this volume, or any other creative work I do, would not exist.

Dad's lifelong work of study and thought have provided throughout my life a wonderful background to discuss ideas and consider possibilities. Without his work as a base, I could not possibly have written this book. As a painter and film-maker, I am grateful for the way Dad has taught me to "see." Mother always was (and is) a haven of creative interest, love and support. They both have my eternal love and gratitude.

I would like to thank Jim Buchfuehrer, my partner, friend, and producer, for his friendship, support, and for the endless stimulating conversations we have had over the last years. His friendship and conversation have been invaluable to the development of the ideas in this book.

Many thanks to my good friend Ray Cioni, with whom I have spent many many pleasant working hours on various film projects and other creative endeavors. His understanding of the creative process, and what goes into it, has helped to form the content expressed here.

Kurt Mitchell deserves special thanks for the wonderfully imaginative cover and interior illustrations for this book. His visual wit perfectly complements the text.

I would like to mention in loving memory Dr. Hans Rookmaaker, for the stimulation and encouragement he gave me during the years I was beginning to paint. Our many talks together, and his support of my artistic endeavors from my early childhood on, were a constant source of help. In writing this book, I have sorely missed having him to call upon for his advice, counsel and the pleasure of his friendship.

Lastly, I would like to thank Susie Skillen for her help in editing the 1985 revised edition of this book.

INTRODUCTION

Whenever Christians, and evangelicals in particular, have attempted to "reach the world" through the media—TV, film, publishing and so on—the thinking public gets the firm idea that, like soup in a bad restaurant, Christians' brains are better left unstirred.[1]

The reasons for this unfortunate state of affairs are several. This book does not attempt to deal with all of them. However, in this small volume I have pinpointed one particular area which has had an outsize influence on our ability as Christians to communicate to the world around us and, more important, our ability to truly enjoy God and our fellow human beings.

This is the area of appreciation, activity, thought, and action, which I will loosely describe as "the arts." By "the arts," I do not mean only the "high arts," but all the range of human expression—from the way we decorate our homes all the way to Michelangelo's *David*, from the most humbly penned letter to the writing of William Shakespeare.

As Christians we often speak of men being "made in God's image." This formula only remains a set of words until given further meaning and definition. If there is one area that surely sets man clearly apart from

[1]See further comments on P. G. Wodehouse from which this is roughly paraphrased.

11

the rest of the animal kingdom and gives meaning to these words "made in the image of God," it is the area of creativity, the capacity to enjoy beauty, to communicate artistically and through abstract ideas.

The area of creativity therefore is no minor footnote to the Christian life, but is an essential. The trouble is, much of the church, for reasons herein described, have forgotten how central this part of our life is and have therefore wound up poverty-stricken in the enjoyment of themselves, their fellow human beings and above all, God himself. It is in the hope that this problem can be addressed and corrected that I offer you this volume.

I wish most particularly that those of you with creative abilities yourselves or an interest in creativity, who have been so consistently ignored by the church, will find encouragement from this book.

Finally, may I draw your attention to the structure of this book. First are the Chapters as Part One. Second the Question and Answers section as Part Two. Both form the whole and are equally important to the argument set forth herein.

Franky Schaeffer V

PART ONE

The Chapters

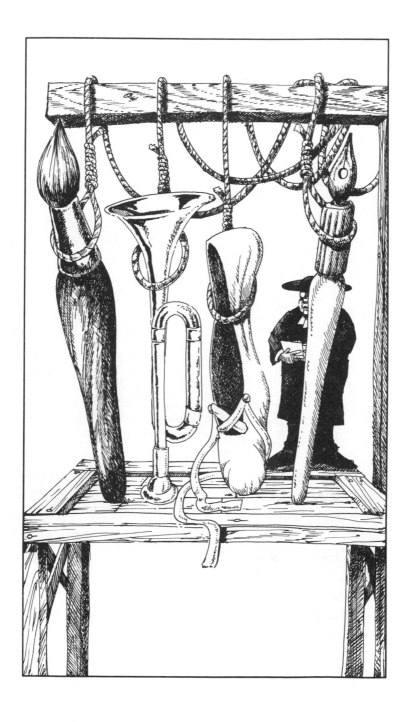

1 CREATIVITY AND BEAUTY

Until the return of Christ and the restoration of all things, that group of believers through history known as the church of Christ will never achieve perfection in any one day and age.

Each age has its blind spots, some generations in church history more than others. The church's effectiveness in the world is stifled proportionate to the extensiveness of its blind spots.

Each generation of the church has its own blind spots peculiar to the age in which it lives. These usually come from some sort of unwitting adaptation to or infiltration of the problems of the society around the church into the church itself. So, for example, one can think of the proabortion ideas certain portions of the church hold as a direct result of being infiltrated by the low view of human life around the church during this day and age.

Sadly, the church often seems to twist and manipulate biblical teachings, usually out of context, to support secular views of its day which it already holds. Sometimes this acceptance is deliberate because of convenience and a desire to fit in to surrounding culture without too much discomfort. Sometimes this infiltration occurs subconsciously over a long period of time. The church also is weakened from within. Often it sets up its own human traditions in opposition to biblical truth.

But always the price paid for being infiltrated (from inside or outside) is one that prevents the church from carrying out its responsibilities.

While church history affords an interesting study from which we can draw many useful lessons, nevertheless it is idle to lament the past if we are not willing to examine the blind spots of our own era which prevent our being effective Christians.

The arts, cultural endeavors, enjoyment of the beauty of both God's creation and of man's creativity—these creative gifts have in our day been relegated to the bottom drawer of Christian consciousness, despised outright as unspiritual or unchristian. This deficiency has been the cause of many unnecessary guilt feelings and much bitter fruit, taking us out of touch with the world God has made, with the culture in which we live, and making us ineffectual in that culture.

The best of the traditional view of the church, supported by biblical teaching, has been (thankfully) that the arts, creativity, enjoyment of our own creativity, the creativity of those around us—in short, all the beauty that God has put into this life—comes as a direct good and gracious gift from our Heavenly Father above. Thus the arts, the enjoyment of them, all these expressions of man's creativity and ability to communicate, need no justification—they need no spiritual justification, and they need no utilitarian justification. They are what they are.

If from this world around us we can learn anything about God's character, surely it is that he is creative and diverse, a God whose interest in beauty and
detail must be unquestioned when one looks at the
world he has made around us, and particularly people
themselves as the result of his craftsmanship.

We could live in a flat uninteresting world, one
that had the bare minimum of gray ingredients to support life, one whose diversity was only enough to provide the minimum of existence. Instead, we live in a
riotous explosion of diversity and beauty. We live in a
world full of "useless" beauty, millions of species, and
individuals of infinite variety, talents, and abilities. And
this is only on our own planet. When one looks heav-
enward and sees the complexity of the reaches of space
above us, the mind boggles at the creativity of our
God.

All this does not even take into account the un-
seen world around us, which the Bible tells us is there;
its richness and creative interests remain to be discov-
ered. As if this were not enough, God has given us in
written form a volume which spans all the human
emotions, the ups, the downs, the diversity of individuals, the good with the bad, the ugly, the beautiful, the
sinners, the righteous, the perverted, the saved, the
lost, the poetry, the poets, the wisdom, the wise, the
human stories, the reality of life, pregnant with meaning, a book in fact of truth, not pale, narrow, religious
sayings.[1]

Why do I so emphasize this creative and diverse
aspect of our God? Simply because as Christians, all we

are and do is surely based in our Heavenly Father himself, and our ultimate meaning is derived from the meaning which he has invested in us as his image-bearers.

With this high view of creativity and all the things that come from it, it is no wonder that the church (up to our own recent era) while having other blind spots, usually, with a few exceptions, took a high view of the arts and creativity. Instead of rejecting them or barely noticing and taking account of them, she embraced the arts and man's creative abilities (what he makes with his mind and hands) as part and parcel of God's good gift to us as his image-bearers.

It is therefore no surprise to look at the history of the West and Christian culture and see its unrivaled heritage in the arts. It is no coincidence that this tremendous heritage of the arts, this involvement with creativity, also coincided with what we call a Christian consensus. One can reasonably affirm that this Christian consensus owed its existence (at least in part) to the fact that Christians and the church were involved in the arts and the media of their day and age. For the arts—the vehicle of human expression—are the root of all ideas, and ideas are the foundation on which history is built. Cultural endeavors, the arts, and the media are truly the marketplace of ideas. Christians for many centuries dominated creative expression; they embraced it, enjoyed it, cared for it, and exulted in it as a manifestation of God's gift to men. It is no coincidence that they also dominated the culture in which they lived, that there was a Christian consensus.

The list of Christians involved in the arts and human expression through history is almost endless and would form many volumes in itself. Bach, van Eyck, Vermeer, Handel, Mendelssohn, Haydn, Shakespeare, the artists of the early Italian Renaissance, many many hundreds, perhaps even thousands of artists could be searched out who were either personally Bible-believing Christians themselves, with a real and living faith, or at the very least operated unquestioningly within the Christian consensus, taking strength and shelter from its framework.

The common belief that creativity came from God, was good and needed no justification, could be summed up in the following quote from the great Renaissance art historian Giorgio Vasari, who wrote in his second edition of his *Lives of the Artists* (1558):

> Surely design existed in absolute perfection before the Creation, when Almighty God having made the vast expanse of the universe and adorned the heavens with its shining lights, directed his creative intellect further to clear the air and the solid earth. And then, in the act of creating men, he fashioned the first forms of painting and sculpture in the sublime grace of created things. It is undeniable that men, as from a perfect model, statues and pieces of sculpture and the challenges of pose and contour were first derived and for the first paintings, whatever they may have been, the ideas of softness and of unity, and the clashing harmony made by light and shadow, were derived from the same source. I am sure that anyone who considers the question carefully will come to the same conclusions I have reached above, namely, that the origin of

the arts we are discussing was nature itself and that the first image or model was the beautiful fabric of the world and that the Master who taught us was that divine light infused in us by special grace, which has made us not only superior to the animal creation, but even, if one may say so, like God himself.[2]

It is not surprising that those who had a confident belief that God had created all things, including men whom he had made in his image, produced the Christian Western artistic heritage we have. They saw God as the Author of creativity who had given talents to men to exercise.

Here then was the traditional view which led to such great triumphs in the realm of artistic endeavor and human expression by Christians.

I repeat: art, creative human expression, and the enjoyment of beauty need no justification. The ultimate justification is that they come as a good and gracious gift from God above.

---

[1]In looking at the diversity of the Scripture in its content and form, one can hardly imagine that the Bible has anything to do with the present narrow theological sloganeering aspects of evangelical Christianity. It seems to me that if the Bible had been written along the lines of what much of evangelical Christianity represents today, instead of being the full comprehensive wonderful Book of diversity, beauty, knowledge, truth, wisdom, it would be a three-page pamphlet printed probably in words of one syllable, preferably on pink paper (because pink sells), possibly with a scratch and sniff section on the back to stimulate some spiritual experience while reading it. In contrast, the real Bible, the Word of God, is solid, human, verifiable, divine indeed.

[2]Giorgio Vasari, *The Lives of the Artists*, second edition, trans. George Bull, from the preface, 1558.

2 BITTER FRUIT

Unfortunately, today we are in a very different position than that of Giorgio Vasari as he stood at the end of the High Renaissance. He could look back with admiration and wonder at the achievements of his fellow artists, and also cast his eyes northward from Italy to the great explosion of creativity (beginning with people like Albrecht Dürer) in the Flemish, Dutch and German parts of the world.

Today, as a Christian with a practical interest in the arts and creative human endeavor, as I look around I see a very different picture. Contrast in your mind the reality of a few centuries ago, the Giottos, the Rembrandts, the Bachs, the Handels, the Vermeers, the van Eycks, with the present-day reality.

Today, Christian endeavor in the arts is typified by the contents of your local Christian bookstore-accessories-paraphernalia shop. For the coffee table we have a set of praying hands made out of some sort of pressed muck. Christian posters are ready to adorn your walls with suitable Christian graffiti to sanctify them and make them a justifiable expense. Perhaps a little plastic cube with a mustard seed entombed within to boost your understanding of faith. And as if this were not enough, a toothbrush with a Bible verse stamped on its plastic handle, and a comb with a Christian slogan or

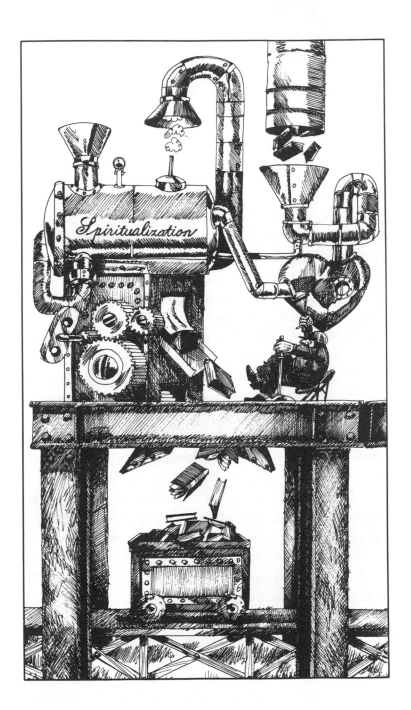

two impressed on it. On a flimsy rack are stacked a pile of records. You may choose them at random blind-folded, for most of them will be the same idle rehash of acceptable spiritual slogans, endlessly recycled as pab-lum for the tone-deaf, television-softened brains of our present-day Christians.

The airwaves as you leave the shop are jammed with a choice avalanche of what can generally be summed up as rubbish, ready to clog your television and radio set with "Christian" programming. The pub-lishing houses churn out (measured by the ton) a land-slide of material which can scarcely be called books, often composed of the same themes which are viewed as spiritual, rehashed by writers who would be better employed in another trade.

In fact, without making the list endless, one could sum up by saying that the modern Christian world and what is known as evangelicalism is marked, in the area of the arts and cultural endeavor, by one outstanding feature, and that is its addiction to mediocrity.

This has borne bitter fruit—in the stifling and destroying of God-given creative instincts in individ-uals, in the false guilt feelings of those with creative talents given by God when they try to exercise those talents in a church which looks at them askance as somehow dabbling in an unspiritual sphere of life. This has produced the unhappy lack of enjoyment of the world around us, of God and man's creativity, and of the fullness of redemption in Christ. And of course the bitterest fruit of this unhappy view of the arts is the erosion of the Christian consensus.

Any group that willingly or unconsciously side-steps creativity and human expression gives up their effective role in the society in which they live. In Christian terms, their ability to be the salt of that society is greatly diminished.

3 "SPIRITUALITY" AND "SECULARISM"

There are basically two reasons why an individual or a group makes some terrible mistake. One is outright stupidity and an inability to grasp the issue; the second is a false view of truth at some particular point—in other words the wrong foundation, the wrong principles, the wrong presuppositions.

In looking at the Christian world around us, one is tempted to believe that the first is the case. The behavior in the area of the arts and the media has caused some intelligent people to reject Christianity outright on their observing of this phenomenon. It seems at times, in the areas we are discussing, that the Christian community, the evangelical establishment, often exhibit to the world an I.Q. about thirty points lower than that of a rather demented jellyfish.

But upon reflection I think it is probably more true to say that the present tragic disinterest—in fact, the anticultural, antiartistic feeling of the church today—comes from a misunderstanding of biblical truths and Christianity as they apply to the arts. This misunderstanding did not arise all at once and cannot be traced to one individual or heretic. However, it did develop in two specific ways.

The first is what I will call a theological development, the second a secular development.

In the nineteenth and early twentieth centuries (in Protestant circles), a strange truncated unscriptural view of spirituality grew up. First spirituality was seen as something separate from the rest of real life. It was above ordinary things; it was cut off from the everyday working out of our lives. Spirituality became something religious and had a great deal less to do with truth, daily life, and the application of Christian principles through that life. It became something in itself, both the means to an end and the end in itself. Spirituality became a thing separated from the rest of life. Thus, certain things increasingly were regarded as spiritual and other things as secular.

The true division in the Christian life between one group of activities in life and another is that line we call sin. Those things which are specifically sinful are indeed cut off and separate from the rest of life for Christians and to be avoided, but everything else comes under the heading of our Christian life, if it is to be a true and full Christian life in the real sense. Either Christ has redeemed the whole man, including every part of him (except those things that are sinful), or he has redeemed none of them. Either our whole life comes under the Lordship of Christ or no part can effectively come under it.

Either God is the Creator of the whole man, the whole universe, and all of reality and existence, or he is the Creator of none of it. If God is only the Creator of some divided platonic existence which leads to a tension between the body and the soul, the material world and the spiritual world, if God is only the Creator of some spiritualized "praise-the-Lord" feeling, then he is not much of a God. Indeed, he is not I AM at all. When our Christianity is allowed to become merely spiritual and inward without the incarnational and outward expressions of God's presence in the world, our faith is no longer meaningful in all areas of life. This indeed is what happened to Christianity during the twentieth century.

Thus people's lives as Christians became compartmentalized. This thing was spiritual, that one was not. The arts, creativity, enjoyment of beauty, enjoyment of God's beauty, even an enjoyment of God's Word in the Bible for itself, were set aside. The arts were regarded as unspiritual, unfit, and secondary to those high and spiritual goals now set forth for Christians to achieve.

Life was divided into categories and compartments. Worst of all, there became a kind of hierarchy of spirituality. This went far beyond the arts and affected many other areas of Christian life, but it had devastating effects upon the arts, and they were relegated to the Christian basement.

The results were obvious. Creative people in this framework either had to bow and abandon their God-given talent in favor of a man-made theology, or fly for their creative lives. Many did so, and the vacuum left by the disappearance of creative people within the Christian community has been evident in our lack of ability to communicate to the world around us, and the gray sterility of the Christian world.

The second occurrence, which I call secular, took place during the same general historic period. Something happened in the secular world which then deeply affected and infiltrated the Christian church. Following the Darwinian theory of evolution (which led to the concept of the survival of the fittest and the onward, inexorable and merciless march of society, and to nineteenth-century industrial utilitarianism), people began to look at themselves and the world around them in purely utilitarian terms.

So the tree which once had had value, not least of which was its beauty, its shimmering leaves, the dappled shades it cast upon the mossy ground beneath, now only had value because of how many cubic feet of paper could be produced from it. So even man was measured by what he could achieve, produce, earn, contribute, and so on. Not only that, all man's attributes, talents and endeavors had to be justified in some utilitarian way. No longer was it good enough to say that some human attribute was a God-given gift which should be freely enjoyed and given. Now those gifts had to translate themselves into utilitarian usefulness. They had to contribute monetarily or in some other way to the society. They had to become propaganda tools, advertising tools, or monetary earning tools, to be considered useful and therefore tolerated by the church.

The idea that individuals are worth something in themselves, because they were created in the image of God, whatever they could contribute or not contribute, was abandoned. The same was true with regard to individual talents.

Unfortunately, the church itself was infiltrated by

this view. The view was translated into religious terms. Now everything anyone did had to measure up somehow in utilitarian terms in the church. It had to be useful to the onward march of the church. It had to help in its efforts, in its programs, its church growth emphasis week or whatever.

This would be bad enough by itself. Worse, however, was that the standard of usefulness was based on a false view of spirituality, a shrivelled, truncated, narrow view which selected a few things arbitrarily and called them the "Christian life," the "walk with the Lord," my "Christian growth," witnessing, or whatever. This was all that remained of the full Christian life we were redeemed to and these sad standards were used to measure all Christian endeavor for its utilitarian usefulness to the church.

The arts, (along with politics, the media, medical ethics, and many other things), were particularly and bitterly affected, first relegated to the basement of the church as unspiritual and now, whenever they were allowed to see the light of day, demanded to make some useful contribution to that church.

What could be left of the free beauty and creative spirit which God has given us, or of meaningful participation in society or politics? Very little.

4 "IT WAS GOOD" (AND STILL IS)

How strange for the church of Christ that claims to know Truth (the Creator himself), claims to be seen in the eyes of God as worthwhile enough for redemption and the death of Christ—how strange for this group of people who claim such a close relationship, a restored relationship no less, with the Creator himself, to forget and abandon creativity, a God-given gift, and more, to see it, when it is practiced at all, merely as a utilitarian means to an end, part of the professional Christian machinery. Thus in one stroke the church negated a large portion of man's worth as created in God's image and turned blinded eyes toward the great beauty and creativity given by the Creator himself. The biblical position is so very different.

"In the beginning God created the heavens and the earth. Now the earth was formless and empty, darkness was over the surface of the deep, and the Spirit of God was hovering over the waters. And God said, 'Let there be light,' and there was light. *God saw that the light was good,* and he separated the light from the darkness. God called the light 'day' and the darkness he called 'night.' And there was evening, and there was morning—the first day.

"And God said, 'Let there be an expanse between the waters to separate water from water.' So God made the expanse and separated the water under the expanse from the water above it. And it was so. God called the expanse 'sky.' And there was evening, and there was morning—the second day. And God said, 'Let the water under the sky be gathered to one place, and let dry ground appear.' And it was so. God called the dry ground 'land,' and the gathered waters he called 'seas.' *And God saw that it was good.* Then God said, 'Let the land produce vegetation: seed-bearing plants and trees on the land that bear fruit with seed in it, according to their various kinds.' And it was so. The land produced vegetation: plants bearing seed according to their kinds and trees bearing fruit with seed in it according to their kinds. *And God saw that it was good.* And there was evening, and there was morning—the third day.

"And God said, 'Let there be lights in the expanse of the sky to separate the day from the night, and let them serve as signs to mark seasons and days and years, and let them be lights in the expanse of the sky to give light on the earth.' And it was so. God made two great lights—the greater light to govern the day and the lesser light to govern the night. He also made the stars. God set them in the expanse of the sky to give light on the earth, to govern the day and the night, and to separate light from darkness. *And God saw that it was good.* And there was evening, and there was morning— the fourth day.

"And God said, 'Let the water teem with living creatures, and let birds fly above the earth across the expanse of the sky.' So God created the great creatures of the sea and every living and moving thing with which the water teems, according to their kinds, and every winged bird according to its kind. *And God saw that it was good.* God blessed them and said, 'Be fruitful and increase in number and fill the water in the seas, and let the birds increase on the earth.' And there was evening, and there was morning—the fifth day. And God said, 'Let the land produce living creatures according to their kinds: livestock, creatures that move along the ground, and wild animals, each according to its kind.' And it was so. God made the wild animals according to their kinds, the livestock according to their kinds, and all the creatures that move along the ground according to their kinds. *And God saw that it was good.* Then God said, 'Let us make man in our image, in our likeness, and let them rule over the fish of the sea and the birds of the air, over the livestock, over all the earth, and over all the creatures that move along the ground.' So God created man in his own image, in the image of God he created him; male and female he created them. God blessed them and said to them, 'Be fruitful and increase in number; fill the earth and subdue it. Rule over the fish of the sea and the birds of the air and over every living creature that moves on the ground.' Then God said, 'I give you every seed-bearing plant on the face of the whole earth and every tree that has fruit with seed in it. They will be yours for food. And to all the beasts of the earth and all the birds of the air and all the creatures that move on the ground—everything that has the breath of life in it—I give every green plant for food.' And it was so. *God saw all that he had made, and it was very good.* And there was evening, and there was morning—the sixth day" (Genesis 1, NIV, italics mine).

Repeated more than any other sentence in the whole creation account, what do we see? God affirming the goodness of what he had made. Without strings attached, without utilitarian motives, without church growth programs, without all the activity and trappings with which we so encumber our view of beauty, nature and creativity, we simply see the statement that he looked at what he had made *and saw that it was good.*

Thus from the very first chapter of the Bible, we see creativity in its proper framework. This theme continues through the Bible. Think of the Song of Solomon, the wisdom of Proverbs (that in and of itself is seen as something good and righteous), the many biblical accounts of human interest, the poetry of the Psalms, the abstract "useless" beauty of the Tabernacle, the Temple, the teachings and absolutes of Scripture, the teachings of Christ himself, the ecstatic, human, sensuous, and artistic merit of the Bible.

The Bible, to sum it up, is the last book interested in utilitarianism and propaganda. It is rather the book of truth in which things have great value in themselves, because they are God-given. They need no further justification. There are no religious events in the Bible, only historical events of religious significance. Let me quote Jeremy C. Jackson.[3]

> The trouble with mere religiosity is that it is safely located in space and time outside the rhythm of life. . . . Christ is a living contradiction to this mentality: he

made his grave with the wicked and as risen he ate breakfast. There is no "religious" truth. Either truth is truth or it isn't. And if it is, all of life is involved on the same level. Be circumcised in the heart as well as the flesh, said Isaiah. "Whatever you do, do all to the glory of God," advised Paul (1 Cor. 10:31). The heresy that reflects the human instinct for separating the "sacred" from the "profane" always pretends that you can live life to the full, religiously and humanly, just so long as you do not confuse the two realms. Hypocrisy is not a bad word to describe it.

This of course does not mean that the Christian, the Bible itself, and God himself are not interested in fruit, the results, the effect following the cause. But the results and the hoped for fruit must never be confused with our primary motivation. The clearest example of this can be seen in man's worth. We all hope that in our lives we do something worthwhile, but whether we do something worthwhile or not, our worth is guaranteed in the fact that it rests in the living God himself, having created us in his image. So in every area of life and talent, the same applies.

[3]Jeremy C. Jackson, *No Other Foundation* (Westchester, Ill.: Crossway, 1980), p. 36.

5 WHAT CAN WE DO?

Creativity, human worth, the arts, cultural endeavor, the media, communication, enjoyment of beauty and creativity in others, enjoyment of our own creativity, enjoyment of God's creativity—all of these need no justification. They are good and gracious gifts from the Heavenly Father above. This, like so much of biblical teaching, brings tremendous freedom—not guilty, backward-looking fear, but freedom. Freedom that is brought through Christ's redemption, to go fuller, to go deeper, to go broader, to enjoy more—not to go narrower and narrower into an ever-shrinking, hyped up gloomy little world of spiritual experience.

Christians, of all people, should be those who manifestly apply what they believe in such a way that it frees them to truly see the God-given worth in things that they really have. And if this is so for nature and objects in the world around us, how much more so for our fellow human beings and their creative talents which God has given them. Things do not need spiritual or theological justification. They are what they are—as God made them.

We as Christians are the sons of God himself, not narrow-minded ideologists, measuring everything in a secular ideological framework. Neither must we enslave ourselves to Christian theological propaganda and spiritualization of all reality. We are those who have been freed to see the world truly as it is and to enjoy and revel in the diversity and beauty that God has made. It is from this framework alone that the reverse side of enjoyment, and that is true compassion for our fellow human beings, can come. For only if we fully recognize, appreciate and enjoy the worth of individuals can we have true compassion for individuals who are being deprived of some of their God-given rights and abilities as human beings. "To perceive tragedy is to wring from it beauty and truth."[4]

To return once again to the main theme—what can be done? There are several specific things. First, Christians must free themselves from the misconception of more than a century that everything must be measured in terms of its usefulness to the cause of Christianity.

This need to abandon such a utilitarian view applies equally to both the right and left of the Christian world. Both, for their own reasons, are highly utilitarian in their view of reality, the arts and media. Everything cannot be measured by the amount of sloganeering we do. Everything cannot be measured in church growth programs, or the number of souls saved as if we were chalking up sales of secondhand cars on some great blackboard in the sky.

God has given intrinsic worth to individuals and what they do in and of themselves. All must not be measured in even a spiritualized utilitarianism.

Secondly, we must realize that this truncated view of spirituality that places some things on a higher plane than others, that makes a strange hierarchy within the Christian world, is false.

Odd phrases have crept into the Christian vocabulary, a little private Christian language in itself, which so clearly points up to the problem. Words such as "full-time Christian service" have crept in. What is full-time Christian service? Are the rest of the Christians part-time Christians? What do all these slogans mean? What is this strange hierarchical Christian life? What is our walk with the Lord? What do all these phrases mean when cut off from real life, real existence, real worth, real beauty, real enjoyment? In a vacuum they are merely what they sound like and so often are—spiritual babblings of those addicted not to biblical Christianity, but to mediocrity.

We must get our basic thinking and presuppositions right on this point, if we are to change anything in the area of the arts and creativity. "Art," as my departed good friend Dr. Rookmaaker wrote, "needs no justification." Having this basic presupposition, we must actively resist the avalanche of mediocrity coming to us in the form of Christian "arts" and propaganda. Why is there so much of this stuff? Simply because man, Christian or non-Christian, is created in the image of God, and a vacuum, formed in his soul by denying the God-given arts their proper place, has to be filled by something. He has an inward emptiness. But without the proper base, man fills the void with only twisted, pale shadows of what art could be. This is why we face a torrent of mediocre media-artistic propaganda.

The church tolerates this because there is a strange double standard between what we call the real world (our everyday lives) and our spiritual world. We accept in our spiritual world a mediocrity that would be immediately intolerable in what we regard as the real world, which Christians still live in, even though they try at times to pretend they are having heaven on earth.

Imagine you wish to build a home and for one reason or another you seek out for yourself a "Christian builder." I'm not sure what you would mean by a "Christian builder." Are the bricks he uses Christian? Does he have Bible verses scribbled on them? Perhaps he employs seminary students at slave wages. But for whatever reason you have decided he is a "Christian builder," you employ him, hoping to get a decently constructed house as a result.

You move into your house some months or years later and on the first night of your occupancy, as the rain pours down, torrents of water come through the roof, the refrigerator falls into the basement, the stairs collapse as your wife climbs them, your children receive electric shocks in the shower. You pick up the phone and (if it is still working) call your "Christian builder" and have very strong words with him.

If all he could offer were some spiritual platitudes, perhaps humming a bar of "Jerusalem" to you, quoting a few Bible verses for comfort, telling you that "you were being tested, this is really good for you and you should give thanks in all things," if this was all he

could offer you to console you for having completely ripped you off in the construction of your home, you would be furious.

You see, the mediocrity and platitudes would no longer fit the bill. They would be used to do something in the real world to patch your home, to mend your angered feelings, and they could not accomplish it (bumper stickers are notoriously bad for patching roofs). We would not accept the mediocrity in some real area that we accept daily in the insults of the so-called Christian arts and media, Christian thinking and spiritual world.

In the real world, you run head-on into reality if you try to fly in its face. However, as the arts are less tangible, it is easier to get away with the addiction to mediocrity in them.

But I put it to you that one can get a new house and rebuild a building, but one cannot easily rebuild our minds, or the image of God that we have in those minds, and it is to the mind and soul that the arts speak. It is more serious to accept mediocrity (leaking roofs, floors that do not hold) in the area of the arts and ideas than it is in the physical world. The price we pay is high.

The price is the ludicrous defacing of God's image before the world. The price is abusing and manipulating God-given talents by turning them into mere useful tools. The price is looking only for cheap shortcuts to the fruit without considering the means of getting there. In other words, the price is the integrity of Christians themselves. This leads to Christianity looking ridiculous. The world quite sensibly wants no part of it; after all, "only lunatics vie for failure" (Selzer).

We must resist this avalanche of rubbish. There are exceptions, of course, but too few. The general direction is to fill the vacuum (left by the departure of real creative talents which have been so subverted) with this rubbish. And because it is being done by those who often are, or at least claim to be, fellow-believers, these monstrous commercials for Christ are accepted as Christian art, Christian media, Christian music, Christian writing.

There are no valid excuses for accepting this medi ocrity. The excuse that "sometimes people are saved" is no excuse at all. People have been saved in concentration camps because God can bring good from evil, but this does not justify the evil.

The idea that "the Spirit can work somehow," that God can bring something out of it if we just sort of throw it out there, is unjustifiable from those who claim to know the living God and can see his integrity and dedication to quality in his Word and the world around us. The excuse that "many people see this," and that "somehow it must do some good" and "it's better than nothing" is no excuse. Since when has quantity been the deciding factor with God? Where is the still small voice of integrity? Many people look at the worst in TV; does this justify it? What were Christ's ratings? Many people look at pornography; does this justify pornography? Of all people, Christians should be *addicted to quality and integrity* in every area, not be looking for excuses for second-best.

We must resist this onslaught. We must demand higher standards. We must look for people with real creative integrity and talent, or we must not dabble in these creative fields at all.

All of this does not mean that there is no room for the first halting steps, for experimentation, for mistakes and for development. But it does mean that there is no room for lazy, entrenched, year after year established mediocrity, unchanging and unvaried.

The present trend of Christian television is scandalous in its abandonment of quality, its adoption of sloganeering in place of true values, its repetitiveness and its smarmy unreality—the eternal slick "fundraisin'-God-praisin' smile."

The trend of Christian publishing is the same, although there are more exceptions in this field because it is more easily accessible to the individual writer. The same poor quality is evident in so-called Christian films. They often only have one connection with good films being made, and that is that they use movie cameras and celluloid. Other than that, they have no relationship at all.

The usual practice of the Christian media companies is to measure their potential for effectiveness-outreach in the dollar value of their equipment, not talent, not ideas, not integrity.

When are Christians going to look at the tremendous heritage the Christian church has and reawaken the sleeping giants of creativity within that heritage, who are there, sleeping a forced sleep, having been abandoned by the church? When are Christians going to demand something better? When are we going to stop accepting this mediocrity? Why the guilty support of this stuff? Some have a feeling that we "owe it to the cause." What cause? Surely these things cannot be confused with the cause of Christ?

Christian individuals and the church can reawaken their interest in creativity, in enjoyment of beauty, enjoyment of others' creativity, and enjoyment of God's creativity. This can manifest itself individually, in Christians who no longer feel guilty and unspiritual about what they are doing in the arts, who no longer allow questions such as "what's Christian about that?" to bother them, who realize that all human endeavor is Christian (if it is not sin) and has its roots in God's good grace. Christians can without guilt feelings enjoy, appreciate, express, protest, interrelate with the world around us and our own feelings, those individuals close to us, and the society in general.

We do not need to justify our endeavors by tacking on a few Christian slogans at the end to somehow redeem them. Christ redeems what we do. We do not need to redeem our work with slogans. There is no Christian world, no secular world; these are just words. There is only one world—the world God made.

The arts must be encouraged in ourselves and in others. It often does not take much. History is full of those who, but for the support of one other individual, would have failed in their creative endeavors.

It does not even have to be financial support, though I hope it would be that too. Often an encouraging word, an open interest in what someone is doing

with his creativity, is enough to help that person have the courage to continue with his creative and artistic battles.

To encourage those in the creative area, we must know something about creativity. We must be those who have a great interest in creativity. Whether it is creativity from Christians or non-Christians, all people (saved or unsaved) are made in the image of God, all people are worth the respect that that statement accords them, all people's creative endeavors should interest us. Does this mean that we become experts in the arts in every field? No. But it does mean that there is something drastically wrong if we have no interest in any area of human creativity. Some of us would be more interested in film, others in painting, others in music, others in poetry, literature, writing, dance, sculpture, all marveling at the creativity of God himself in nature around us. But each of us should have a great interest in both what God has made and what man makes as one of God's creatures, and therefore as an expression of God himself.

Christians should be those least threatened of all by new artistic ideas, by experimentation, by taking risks, by looking at and enjoying what the other side has to say. If indeed our feet are solidly rooted on truth itself, we are those who can look the world in the eye with confidence, pleasure, fulfillment.

So often people live in tension between their spiritual activities and the rest of their lives. But Christianity should be a freeing experience which opens our arms to enjoy more of God's world, and in doing so to understand the worth of every human being. In turn we should have more interest, love, and compassion for our neighbor. Amongst others things, equally important, this leads to a greater desire to tell one's neighbor the Good News, not a lessening of that desire.

After all, when we are saved, we are saved to something besides merely the privilege of running around in guilt-motivated frenetic Christian activity trying to save others!

The situation becomes a case of sheep saving more sheep, so that they can save more sheep, so they can save more sheep. The point is missed altogether.

People are saved *to something*, to a rich fullness of life within Christ—not only in heaven, but here and now. Much of this fullness of life comes from a better understanding of ourselves and other people as creative children made in the image of a creative God.

We must support the arts. Churches should support the creative people within the community, not always trying to make them justify what they are doing in some spiritual sense, not demanding sloganeering, not only recognizing their creativity when it can be useful to them, or used on a program, but enjoying it for what it is, a God-given gift.

Christian individuals must change their view of the arts and begin to embrace them once again. The artist, the Christian creative person, far from being driven from the church as somehow a second-class citizen, must once again be embraced and be made welcome, as he or she is.

The church does not always have to financially officially support the arts, but surely the other extreme of having abandoned them altogether and indeed having snubbed them is a sinful denial of God and his creatures.

⁴Richard Selzer, *Mortal Lessons* (New York: Simon & Schuster, 1974).

6   TRUE SPIRITUALITY (REVISITED)

To put my previous chapter in a wider context, let us look for a moment at the way in which some of these principles apply in a few other avenues of life.

Consider the child, embittered against and terrified of Christianity, because he or she has been abandoned by a father and mother busy doing "the Lord's work." The child sits in the day-care center, or at home in front of the TV set, while his or her parents run around doing spiritual things. Yet, what could be more spiritual than to carry out God's commands to love and care for one's own children, to enjoy them, to appreciate them, to celebrate life with them?

Consider the guilt-ridden businessman, wondering what he can do for God, having been sold a Christianity which applies only to certain narrow spiritual confines, having been given the distinct feeling that he must do some Christian activity on the side of his secular business to justify his existence as a Christian (or at the very least write a million-dollar check for some worldwide evangelical program). He does not realize that Christ has redeemed the whole man, that it is precisely in his own area of endeavor, *his business*, that he can make a difference if he quietly applies the principles of Christianity to it, over the long term.[1]

In this context, Martin Luther said that the cobbler praises God when he honestly makes a good pair of shoes.

Christ has redeemed the whole man; Christ has redeemed us as we are.

Consider the two tax collectors of the New Testament, Zacchaeus and Matthew. Christ called one to be an apostle; Christ told the other to go back and collect taxes honestly. Did Christ then go on and point out that Matthew's calling was higher, more spiritual? No, each one of us has a responsibility to God to exercise our own talents in his or her particular area. There is no blueprint for our life. God does not have a "wonderful plan for your life," in the sense that there is a spiritual blueprint he will unroll for you.

He deals with each one of us as individuals, where we are. He has given us the talents we have. God is not a dilettante game-player, who gives us one set of talents and then somehow makes us justify our spirtual lives by calling us to give them up. Each person is an individual. Either the whole man is redeemed by Christ or none of him! Christianity is sensible and down to earth, not some spiritual, "Spirit-filled" game!

Consider John the Baptist's common-sense advice to the soldier, not to be greedy, not to demand more wages, not to extort money from people, and to apply his teaching *where he was* at that time. John did not use some high-falutin' spiritualized theological jargon, some socialist third-world program, some spiritual emphasis week.

The commands of Christ can and should be carried out in daily life. Spirituality unconnected with real existence is like a car in neutral endlessly revving, going nowhere, while the occupants pat themselves on the back and delight at the speed at which the engine is turning over.

Activity for activity's sake is what marks present Christianity. It is going nowhere. If, as the press says, there are millions of evangelical Christians, where is the evidence? Noting all the Christian activity, the money spent, raised, used, the programs, the bumper stickers, the national efforts, the magazines, why then is the culture moving at such devastating speed in an anti-Christian direction? Why is America a pagan state? It is because so often our activities are unconnected to redeeming man where he really is in real life and to applying these principles to the areas that really count today—creativity, society, law, politics, art, etc.

Mediocrity shows up in the standard preaching and teaching of the church, as well as in the attitude toward creativity. If life and spirituality are separated, then even in the churches' primary functions mediocrity reigns supreme.

The level of teaching in the church today reflects this. Since spirituality is seen as an end in itself, what does it matter if sermons become endless repetition of theological jargon that takes the place of truth? As long as it all sounds spiritual, it is accepted. The constant exhortations to "pull up our spiritual socks" and calls to "love" naturally have a hollow ring. They are often only exercises in futile spirituality and remain unapplied to real life and the areas that count.

What can be more truly spiritual in this antifamily

age than a father romping on the carpet with his three-year-old son or daughter?

What can be more spiritual in this sad and often ugly world than the creation of beauty, of art?

What can be more spiritual than the care and love of another individual?

What can be more spiritual than looking at the beauty around us that God has made, with thanksgiving in our hearts?

What can be more spiritual than the care of the orphan and the widow, of the unborn?

What can be more spiritual than loving your husband or wife?

What can be more spiritual than sermons that truly teach? (a rare event).

What can be more spiritual than standing for life in an amoral society—standing for the rights of the child who is going to be aborted, standing for the rights of the unwanted child who is going to be eliminated through infanticide, standing for the rights of the elderly, fighting for a Christian revolution in a secularist pagan state?

What can be more spiritual indeed than living a whole and abundant life before the face of the Lord?

True spirituality is obeying the commands of Scripture and effecting change in the real world, not hiding behind religious experience.

7 FREE TO BE HUMAN

And now a word to my fellow artists and those employed or hoping to be employed in some professional capacity in the arts, fields of expression and communications, and also those who, while living in different professions, have artistic and creative urges and interests personally (therefore, I trust, everyone).

"The world had many kings, but only one Michelangelo," said his contemporary Aretino.

Do not be discouraged. History is on your side. God has given you a talent. You are important to him and live in the court of God, not the court of men. You cannot wait for the Sanhedrin's approval.

By expressing yourself as an artist and by exercising those talents God has given you, you are praising him. Whether what you express is "religious" or "secular," as a Christian you are praising him. Everything is his.

The church's narrow-minded attitude toward the arts, the demand for slogans and justification, the utilitarianism, the programs, the guilt-ridden view of all life is unchristian, unbiblical, ungodly and wrong. Do not let this suppress you, as a member of this generation of creative people, the way it has suppressed so many in the recent past. You must press on.

Remember that as a creative person, the important thing is to create. Who sees what you make, where it goes and what it does is a secondary consideration; the first is to exercise the talent God has given you.

You cannot expect too much too soon. It is the lifelong body of work that counts. It is that body of work whose expression bears fruit by changing the cultures in which we live. One individual work cannot say everything.

Your work will vary, one day to express something rather important to you personally and perhaps less important to the world around you, perhaps another time to wrestle with a weighty issue. There is no right or wrong method. There is no Christian or unchristian subject matter (except in the area of art work or expression that would deliberately have as its primary purpose to lead people away from truth).

You are tremendously free, you are the most free, for you have form on which to build your freedom, you know who you are, you know where your talent comes from, you know that you and your talent will live forever. You know that God has placed worth on you; you know creativity, unlike so many things in this fallen world, did not come from the Fall, but was something there with God before he created, with him when he created, and that he has given to man as his creature. It will be there in the new heavens and the new earth. Your creative talent, exercised and worked on in this life, is something you will take with you. Unlike money, or spiritual slogans, it is eternal.

Produce, produce, produce! Create, create, create! Work, work, work! That is what we must do as Chris-

tians in the arts, with or without the support of the church, if we are to exercise our God-given talent, praise him through it, enjoy it, bear fruit in the age in which we live.

It is a worthwhile fight, and more than a fight it is an enjoyment of a good and gracious gift from our Heavenly Father, freely given, to be enjoyed, practiced, and treasured.

When you get discouraged as a Christian in the arts, consider your heritage. Bathe in the knowledge that for centuries Christians have practiced and nurtured the arts with faithfulness, and that you now carry his torch forward. Take courage from this. Take courage from the creativity and beauty of God's world around us. Take courage from the creativity of other people. Take courage from Solomon's temple.

If any single group of people are in tune with God himself, certainly it is those Christians who enjoy, practice or simply appreciate creativity.

Creativity is not a committee endeavor. Creativity does not fit very well with a socialistic concept of life. Creativity is individual, just the way God made us. It is an individual expression, it is your expression.

There are only two kinds of art, good art and bad art. There is good secular art and bad secular art. There is good art made by Christians and bad art made by Christians (and all the shadings in between).

There is no such thing as Christian art any more than there are Christian bricks for the house builder. Naturally your whole lifetime body of work will express something of who you are as a person, including what you think, but for many this will often be far more subconscious than conscious.

If you are a real Christian, this will in some way naturally manifest itself in your work, maybe now, maybe later, but the point is to get on and do what you are doing, not to worry about every stroke of the brush as if it was a philosophical treatise.

Whether your album has enough "Christian" cuts on it or not is not the point. Get on with what you are doing, being thankful for your gift. It is as simple as that.

[1]See George Gilder's book *The Spirit of Enterprise* (New York: Simon & Schuster, 1984) for a wonderful study of what creativity and freedom, given by God, can mean when applied to commerce and business.

8 THE REAL CHRISTIAN LIFE

The Christian life is not guilt-ridden, backward-looking, sloganeering, bubble-gum, theological poster muck. The Christian life is full enjoyment of God himself, those around us (saved or not), and their talents. The Christian life exhibits a deepening appreciation of all God has made, a growing longing to understand and enjoy what is around us, and the desire to stand for those godly principles of life, beauty, truth, enjoyment and justice so clearly given us in the Bible.

May we each struggle in our own areas to apply the broad and wonderful truth of Christianity to what we are doing, and not merely make ourselves "useful to the cause."

May we have the courage to reject and abandon the mediocrity of the church today and stand alone if need be.

May we stand up for life, art, love, family, children, and compassion in an antilife, prodeath world.

May we lead a richer life brought to us through Christ. May our Christianity be a freeing experience, not an ideological burden. May we experience a freedom from guilt feelings, a willingness to take risks, make mistakes, but above all to live the life God has given us, within the bounds of his absolutes.

The Christian life does not call for us to deny our

God-given nature. The Christian life does not call us to deny the creative nature of God himself. We must deny sin. Indeed, we must fight evil at every turn. *But we must afirm life and goodness!*

It is time that we Christians who claim to have such an interest in life after death begin to show some interest in a little life before death.

PART TWO

Questions and Answers

Note Concerning the Question and Answer Section

As Christians struggle with how they should relate to the arts today, they are faced with many questions, some of them immobilizing. The following questions are among those which the author has had to deal with most frequently, but they are also those of greatest interest and importance. These have been raised over the past several years during the author's lecture and seminar tours, as well as in personal conversation and correspondence. The following questions cut to the heart of the issues, while the author's practical answers are directed toward a wide audience. (The Publisher)

Q. Does the addiction to mediocrity you speak of only concern middle-class evangelical churches and people, or does it cut across all of Christendom?

A. This utilitarian view of the arts by Christians in our century and the late nineteenth century led to the idea that unless one was writing a hymn, illustrating a tract, a Christian magazine cover or a missionary pamphlet, one could not be serving God with one's art.

Today we find ourselves in a slightly more complicated position. One school, the traditional pietists, still maintains that the ultimate destiny of every creative Christian is to somehow find an excuse to push his art work into the mold of witnessing evangelization propaganda. The result is the Christian poster with its attendant Christian graffiti to somehow justify it, or the Christian song with its inevitable slogan tacked on at least at the end to justify it, or some other form.

Today we still have this kind of utilitarianism. However, to complicate matters there is a new breed of utilitarianism, which has come about largely through those who (often for correct reasons) have rebelled against the materialistic consumer-oriented utilitarian activity for activity's sake position of the church.

Unfortunately, those who have rebelled have latched on to another nineteenth-century phenomenon and have been infiltrated by it and just as damaged as those they have rebelled against.

These are the ones I would term the Christian new left (represented by those such as Ronald J. Sider, Anthony Campolo, or Nicholas Waltersdorf).

These people, once again, do not see man as a whole, and regard everything as utilitarian. It must fit in with their programs and ideological utopian socialist view of the world. Thus we are right back where we started, only in a different form.[1]

The church, in the creative area and in others, will get nowhere until it realizes that Christianity is itself its own standard, and is a freeing experience, not an ideological bondage. Christianity has no similarities, either with the industrial utilitarianism of the nineteenth century or the reaction to it in the present-day form of socialism, which is a sort of watered down combination of many leftover nineteenth- and twentieth-century ideological attempts at rebellion which have gone nowhere, and often have produced terrible inhumanities.

Christians must affirm their own principles and no others. It is useless trying to combine worn and outdated socialist principles to fill the vacuum left by a truncated, utilitarian, spiritualized view of things.

---

[1]For example, see Anthony Campolo's writing against spending to create beautiful church buildings (in *It's Friday But Sunday's A' comin'*, Waco, Tex: Word, 1984).

Q. Why are mediocre efforts on the part of the Christian media world often so successful?

A. First let me say that success in communication media (books, films, art, etc.) must be measured in the long term. The nineteenth-century Impressionists were mainly failures in their own time. However, they changed the course of art history and their works are the only legitimate survivors of that period.

Secondly, remember that true artistic success is measured against achievement in a given field, not by sales, ratings or funds raised. This has always been the case and should be doubly so for real Christians.

Thirdly, we live in a mediocre, consumeristic, shallow society anyway, where TV sets the standards and priorities. Naturally when Christians mirror that world successfully, they will achieve certain ends. Just as commercial for dandruff shampoos achieve certain ends, these successes cannot be confused with artistic endeavors.

Fourthly, this whole book deals with motivation, integrity, and the intrinsic worth of the creative effort. This is an obvious contradiction of the mentality behind the "success" of the Christian media world today.

Fifth, most of the output in Christian media is aimed at maintaining the evangelical establishment, a whole little subculture with its own writers, journalists, TV hosts, and musicians. Success is measured by comparing the sales and popularity of these inbred artists as they are rewarded by those who populate this little ghetto. Unfortunately, they are rarely matched against accepted objective artistic standards, and the heritage of Western culture.

Many of these people have grown up in the evangelical ghetto and are not even aware of the existence (in real terms) of the whole world God has made out there, either the world of nature or man.[2]

[2]For example, consider the way in which the new "evangelical" left has pathetically managed to only restate the arguments of the 1960s new left and has ignored or been unaware of the neo-conservative movement which has totally debunked the "new left" and its failed socialism.

Q. Could you give a few specific examples of what you call exceptions to the trend toward mediocrity by Christians?

A. Fortunately, there are exceptions. In this century one thinks of C. S. Lewis, of Tolkien, or certain other writers and thinkers such as Francis Schaeffer, Solzhenitsyn, Dorothy Sayers, Walker Percy, and others.

Many of the Christians who are exceptions to this century's rule of mediocrity are those who were already practicing their art form in a secular context (the real world at least has the standard of the marketplace to contend with). When they became Christians, they avoided being submerged by the church and evangelical establishment to remain intact as artists.

Fortunately I know of many lesser known (at least for the moment) creative people in both the United States and Europe, particularly Holland, England and America, who are practicing their art with great faithfulness and skill.

Here are a few examples: in London, there are theater groups (e.g., Upstream Co.); in Holland there are at least a dozen excellent artists and sculptors that I know personally (e.g., Britt Wikström); and in America there are many artists (e.g., Steven Hawley), graphic designers, animators (e.g., Ray Cioni), sculptors, photographers (e.g., Sylvester Jacobs), several young filmmakers and writers who are supporting themselves. In addition, there are a number of fine craftsmen, such as furniture makers (e.g., Jon Ording, a friend and Christian, being perhaps the best alive today in the United States), and poets (e.g., Steve Turner), or writers (e.g., Harold Fickett).

Underlying evidence of the problem discussed in this book is the church's ignorance of these talents; yet it is attentive to the leadership of so many dubious spiritual leaders. These leaders' "talents" seem to range from outright charlatanism and buffoonery to the lunatic fringe heresies of much of the church today. The stuffy complacency of the professional Christian leads the way to an epidemic of Christian divorce and remarriage. In order to gain acceptance, Christian leaders are deliberately blind to the great evils of the day, such as abortion, and refusing to speak out for fear of losing followers.

Q. As a film-maker, how do you see the motion picture as an art form, and how should someone who has neglected appreciating this field catch up?

A. There is no doubt in my mind that one of the genuine high art forms of the twentieth century is cinema. Any real appreciation of today's forms of cultural expression must include in its scope the cinema.

The following short, incomplete, highly personal list contains a few of the feature-length films and directors I have much enjoyed and been enriched by.

> Federico Fellini: *La Strada; La Dolce Vita; Satiricon; 8½; Roma; Amarcord; Prova d'Orchestra (Orchestra Rehearsal)*
>
> Federico Fellini is the maestro of sets, atmosphere, imagination and fantasy. His films are a great and enjoyable collection of visual spectacles.
>
> In addition, his works stand out as the sharpest and most satirical examination of the decadence and decline of a post-Christian culture, moving toward a new paganism.
>
> Fellini is the film-maker's film-maker. He uses the medium to its limits. He is a good example of that great gift and cousin to creativity, *imagination.*
>
> Pier Paolo Pasolini: *A Thousand and One Nights; Oedipus Rex*
>
> Another diverse Italian director. Creates a total atmosphere in his films which to me is spellbinding and dreamlike.
>
> Woody Allen: *Annie Hall; Manhattan; Stardust Memories*

Woody Allen is his own man and while he graciously bows to Groucho Marx and others, he is a real original.

Alan Parker: *Midnight Express;* William Friedkin: *French Connection II;* Francis Ford Coppola: *Godfather II*
These films each represent a particular *genre*. Good examples of entertainment at its very best.

George Lucas: *Star Wars; The Empire Strikes Back; Return of the Jedi*
Star Wars marked the beginning of a hundred imitations. However, technically and considering its budget, it is one of the tightest, best directed productions of recent memory.
(I have enjoyed the opportunity of explaining the difference between the vague pantheistic "Force" in the films and Christian truth to my children.)

Most films by Luis Buñuel, François Truffaut, and Stanley Kubrick are worth watching, as is anything directed by Ridley Scott *(Blade Runner,* etc.).

There are several dozen very good directors and many fine technicians employed in film today. They deserve and will reward your attention.

Film is a great, diverse, human medium. Still in its infancy, cinema is only at its very beginning. We have the honor and privilege to watch it grow and to study the world and ideas through it.

Q. How would you appraise Christian efforts in film in general up to this point?

A. The illiterate repetitive hash of Christian dramatic films is unbelievable. As with most Christian books published today, they could be summed up in a few simple categories which are endlessly and timidly reshuffled: the sob story, the dramatic conversion, before and after ("I used to be high on drugs, but not I'm high on the Lord"), the narrow escape, the testimony (always famous and infamous people), the how to in three easy lessons, and so forth.

The point is not that none of these subjects are worth ever treating and thinking about, but that they are seen to work for the church market and therefore are reused to redundancy. What terrible timidity for those who should have such great confidence! How appalling when compared with the gutsy gist of the Bible itself.

Q. What is the relationship between what you are saying and so-called Christian TV?

A. With particular attention to the United States, the newest in the trend of the strange repertoire of cultural events billed as Christian involvement with the media has been an expanding role of a Christian presence in television.

In all the ups and downs of Christian involvement with the arts and the pitfalls through history, current Christian television is certainly the most loathsome debacle.

Television itself for many reasons is a dubious enterprise. (You must read *Four Arguments for the Elimination of Television* by Jerry Mander, Morrow Quill Paperbacks.)

Christians and Christian imitators, who often are indistinguishable in this fast-growing greasy money field, have adopted the worst of television style, have studiously ignored any creative programming, and pander, as does most TV, to the shallow, the frivolous, the quick fix, and the sensational.

The content of Christian TV is often downright heretical if you're interested in theology (I saw one TV host claim that the satellite he was about to put up to beam his rubbish worldwide was fulfilling biblical prophecy and was one of the angels of the last times that St. John saw). For TV to become any sort of art form or serious attempt at media communication requires a much higher level of programming, greater diversity, and creative imagination.

That the church and individuals subject themselves to, and worse financially support this TV drivel is evidence of the Christian double standard concerning the arts.

Most so-called Christian efforts in television can only congratulate themselves for their massive fundraising efforts and subsidiary money-making empires such as retirement homes, seminaries, and Bible colleges that they are building to spread the risk of their investments. In addition, they boast vast arrays of expensive technical equipment which sometimes rival secular networks in hardware.

Television is the worst and most monolithic example of the mediocrity of the Christian media. Radio and film contain more exceptions, publishing and magazines more yet. As the medium becomes more accessible because of lower costs, the spectrum of participation widens and therefore there are more exceptions to the rule of mediocrity.

Certain Christian TV shows are merely televised church services and can be judged as such, not on the TV value but the content of the teaching. This may be a waste of TV as a medium, but is often less offensive than other shows. In some cases TV has helped push for greater involvement by Christians in politics and society, sometimes achieving good purposes.

"The 700 Club," a TV show of the Christian Broadcasting Network, stands as an exception to the rule. They have begun to use an informative magazine format and through this have examined many pressing issues of the day. The show is well produced.

Q. What room do you allow for individual taste in all these questions?

A. Personal taste and quality should not be confused. To a certain extent we all see things subjectively in all areas of life. This does not mean, however, that there cannot be clear standards.

While we must allow for individual taste, there is such a thing as objective integrity and quality. We must struggle to find this quality, truth and integrity in our work.

Much of the Christian world has adopted the idea that quality and integrity don't even matter. This is not allowing for different taste, this is addiction to mediocrity.

Q. How do economics enter in? Is enjoyment of beauty only for the rich? Is it elitist?

A. Beauty, worth and quality, sensitivity, love, compassion—these are freely given by God and can be freely enjoyed. Economics do not usually enter in, any more than in all of life.

Selecting what we do with sensitivity is as important as what we do not do. Often sensitivity to beauty and creativity will cost less, not more. Most of the time, it is a question of how we spend what we have, not a question of spending more or less.

It is also a question of getting our priorities straight. The cost of a new color TV set would cover many fine original works of art by worthy young artists. The cost of one trip to Disneyland would amply cover a concert season in most cities. The cost of many of the accessories and gadgets of middle-class life today could be equally spent on many soul-enriching artistic experiences and enjoyable times. The cost of a mediocre Christian book could be spent on a fine literary work. The hour you spend in church listening to a lousy sermon could be spent reading the Bible on a great beach.

For those with very little money indeed, or no money, the greatest beauty of all remains free in the natural world God has created around us. Creativity is also expressed in human expression and conversation. These things are free. Enjoyment of much so-called high art is also free. Many museums, retrospectives, even concerts are free of charge or cost very little. Less is often more, and ugly "wood"-plastic paneling will cost more than a plain whitewashed wall against which a print can be hung and exposed to advantage. Often ugliness costs more than the simplicity of beauty.

Without going into further detail then, I feel that economics certainly enters in on some levels of, let us say, art collection, but not in the most fundamental areas of enjoyment of beauty. I can remember with pleasure sitting in the mouth of a Bedouin tent in the Sinai desert, looking at the heat haze shimmering over the rock-strewn landscape as it rolled undulating away to the horizon. I was sitting in a tent of handwoven carded wool of natural colors, on a carpet of brown, and white sheepskin, with a small charcoal fire burning in front of me. On that fire was a simple brass cooking vessel. These were poor people by Western standards. Nevertheless, the natural beauty of their home in the form of the Bedouin tent, the ancient tradition of their culture and their environment were fundamentally more beautiful than most middle-class plastic Christian homes costing hundreds of times more than everything these people would earn monetarily in a lifetime.

Wealth is a byproduct of creativity and freedom anyway. Therefore art, which is one part of creativity, is part of the process that creates abundance for all people. To say one is "for the poor," but be against freedom, creativity, and art is a contradiction of terms. Michael Novak has argued this point well in his book *The Spirit of Democratic Capitalism* (New York: Simon & Schuster, 1982), as have George Gilder and Thomas Sowell in their writings.

85

Q. How do the many church activities of the evan-gelical community fit in with what you are saying?

A. Even in the context of church activities themselves, the church so often divides instead of bringing togeth-er. Ninety-year-olds go to the ninety-year-old class, sev-enty-year-olds to the seventy-year-old class, on down to toddlers who are shunted off away from the rest of the family.

Thus the church splits up the family, mirroring the way the twentieth century divides the family into compartments.

It might be a good idea to abandon our frenetic addiction to church activities altogether in favor of more warm and personal human relationships, which are natural and God-given, within the family and in friendships. After all, for a Christian married couple, making love is as spiritual as some church activity. Isaac took Rebekah to his mother's tent, not to some prayer meeting or spiritual emphasis week.

God in Scripture has left the church for us as an institution to serve a very real and worthwhile pur-pose. However, the constant activity-oriented nature of the church today, which is more like some combination health club-golfing society-bowling tournament-Sun-day school service-inspirational message-fellowship-Je-sus advertising machine-growth program all rolled into one, does not seem to have very much to do with the institution we read about in the New Testament. As mentioned before, the level of teaching is often so shallow, repetitive, and worthless as to be more destructive than helpful.

In the light of what has been said in this book about the division of the spiritual from our real lives, a long hard look at this activity-oriented church of ours would serve a useful purpose.

The fact the church is activity-, experiential- and entertainment-oriented is no coincidence in this activity and entertainment age. But being a Christian does not consist of doing Christian activities that are so often only men's activities dressed up and made almost mandatory by our middle-class church. Don't let the church eat you alive. Stay home and have a family, as well.

Q. How does what you are saying fit in with the biblical call to witnessing and spreading the gospel?

A. Nothing said in this volume should be taken as deemphasizing certain individual God-given natural talents and the call to creatively evangelize as a full-time task in itself. There is no conflict here.

What must be seen, however, is that evangelization has sometimes been narrowed down to a spiritual activity to such an extent that it has become the only form of Christian activity which anyone feels guilt-free to practice.

Evangelization is *always important,* as is the individual call for each Christian to tell the Good News. Nothing in this volume minimizes any of that.

In fact, a proper understanding of the fullness of who man is leads to a greater interest in true evangelization.

God gives many talents, and evangelization is no more spiritual then anything else. Such an understanding broadens rather than narrows, embraces rather than excludes the good parts of existing Christian activity.

Q. What has the rise of the so-called charismatic movement done in terms of the questions you are discussing?

A. Historically, the church back to the earliest times has always had a struggle between the body and the soul, the spiritual and the secular, in seeking to know how to obey God's commands.

But throughout most of church history, this struggle was manifested in the attempt to apply God's truths to one's daily life and profession.

The idea of a Christian hierarchy of values in which the soul is at the top and the body is at the bottom is platonic. The biblical position is that God has made man, body and soul, as a whole.

In our own day and age, the group that has most carried the body/soul tension to its logical and unhappy conclusion has been a new breed of charismatics. Having reduced the Christian life to the realm of feelings and personal experience, they move from one spiritual high to another to validate their Christian faith.

It is no coincidence that in the area of the arts that we are speaking of in this volume, this breed of charismatic teaching has produced the very worst of Christian arts and media. Much of so-called Christian TV exhibits this phenomenon. As experience is primarily the judge of things, the charismatics lack a real basis for enduring standards (theologically or artistically).

Having separated spiritual experience, through slogans and cliché phrases, away from real life and

made it higher than everything else, spiritual experience has been made basically worthless because it is no longer connected to reality.

Thus, we find a rather pathetic guilt-ridden, panic-stricken group of people, stuck on the spiritual treadmill of personal experience as the highest authority, who are constantly having to outwardly reaffirm their spiritual worth.

An introverted little charismatic language has grown up that has its own terms and vocabulary, to constantly make it possible to be instantly recognized as belonging. Terms, jargon, claims of healing, and slogans become almost a passport to acceptance within such groups.

Thus, ironically, often those who claim to be the most exclusively interested in spiritual growth are those who in the end look for the most superficial, mundane, outward signs and surface manifestations of this growth.

The Bible is very different and looks for true spiritual manifestations in the everyday real applications of Judeo-Christian teachings of absolutes, charity, and enjoyment of God. But this is not "spiritual" or exciting enough for some, who seem to want a Christianity that competes with Disneyland.

In addition, the present vogue for end-time fantasies often leaves such people with no real interest in the plight of this world, let alone an interest in the arts.

Q. You are critical of Christians involved in the arts and media. What about the secular world?

A. In this volume, in the spirit of putting our own house in order first, we are primarily considering the "Christian arts" with a sharply critical look at those arts. It would only be fair to add that the world of secular art is in at present total disarray and an unhappy position itself.

This is chiefly because the Western secular world, having lost its roots in its Judeo-Christian past (as far as Western culture goes), has of course paid a similar price as the Christian world, which has also lost its roots in its true Christian heritage.

So we find addiction to mediocrity in the secular world also—much repetition, lack of innovation and stupidity. TV practically consists of nothing else.

But a large segment of the secular world nevertheless maintains a higher standard than the Christian arts and media. This, it seems to me, can be understood simply by the fact that the secular world at least has the standard of the marketplace which it must meet.

The Christian world has not even a poor standard, because it operates on a double standard principle. It judges its spiritual activities, in which it includes its media and arts efforts, by spiritual standards, unlike the standards it applies to the rest of life. Thus an art work, song, or whatever can be highly acclaimed because of its spiritual content, even if it is a miserable exhibition of a lazy addiction to mediocrity, which denies those very spiritual facts it is claiming to proclaim.

In the secular world, this usually simply does not wash, or it will not work and not sell. While the marketplace is a sad standard if it is the only one, as it is often now in the secular world, it is nevertheless better than none, or worse a double standard.

Hopefully, Christians involved in the arts will begin to march to the beat of their own drummer, whose call to a high standard is not on the basis of selling or spirituality, but on the basis of integrity, beauty, content, love, compassion, and all those other Christian fruits which lead us toward an addiction to quality rather than mediocrity.

While the secular world does have much mediocrity in it, its worst sin is its often deliberate bias against Christianity and Christian ethics. To fight this bias effectively and to demand a hearing requires Christian achievement of the highest order. Because of our mediocrity we Christians all too often provide the excuse the world is looking for to ignore the truth of Christianity.

Q. Are there any other examples in history of a period during which the church took an antiart, anticultural stand? Can you be specific?

A. From the time of the Romans up until about 100 years ago, the church, the Christians have generally supported the arts as a God-given gift.

There have been some notable exceptions. For instance, during the history of the Florentine Renaissance, a friar called Fra Girolamo Savonarola of the city of Ferrare stirred quite a following in the days of a corrupt and divided Roman Catholic Church. Along with many rather ascetic teachings, he took a definite antiarts stance, during the time of the famous Sandro Botticelli. There were burnings of paintings, books, and so forth. Indeed, Botticelli himself burned some of his paintings on at least one of these occasions.

Savonarola's followers were referred to as the "*Pignoni,*" which means "the snivelers." Botticelli as a case in point eventually abandoned his artwork altogether in favor of this ascetic sniveling and in his old age had to cast himself upon the munificence of Lorenzo de' Medici to support his most basic needs.

Savonarola's antiart teachings were amongst several of the many ideologies he put forth, which so incensed the people of his day that eventually with popular support he was (with some of his followers) hanged and then burned. Thus the Florentine people of his day displayed uncommonly good common sense as regards an antiarts stance!

There have been other examples pointed to primarily by secular anti-Christian art historians, such as Lord Kenneth Clark in his book and television series *Civilisation*, which have tried to cast disparagement, particularly on the Reformation church as regarding the arts. In particular he points out the image, statue and church ornament destruction of the early Reformation.

These examples, however, are erroneous and misleading, when one realizes that a) the Reformation eventually produced a wealth of art equal to its southern cousin, the Renaissance; b) when these art works were destroyed, they were not destroyed as art works as such or with any antiart feeling, but rather as religious symbols of perceived heresy which the Reformation was standing against for other reasons. Thus, to try and twist these examples into a general proof of antiart sentiment by the Protestant part of the church of that time is an illegitimate critique.

Q. What are some specific examples of Christians and church involvement with the arts in previous history?

A. The beginnings of the early church coincided with the crumbling of the Roman Empire and its artistic achievements and abilities.

The classical Greek and Roman world had achieved great heights in technical ability and artistic achievement. As the Roman Empire dissolved in its own decadence, the arts declined as well.

Out of the ashes of this dissolution came the Christian church which has stood through history down to our own day. The very early Christians in the first small catacomb paintings displayed a great interest in the arts and creativity from the church's earliest days. Some of these expressions were of biblical themes, others of general topics and decorative.

The knowledge of drawing and design, perspective and anatomical structure exhibited in some of these catacomb paintings, as in the Arian church of St. Lorenzo in Milan, are even superior to the later Byzantine period.

As the early church and secular history moved away from the Roman era, and the technical and artistic knowledge of that period was lost, so the Christians of that day, as part of that historical period, also lost their expertise. As a result, the stiff Byzantine spiritualized Eastern style of art was adopted.

Most of the rudimentary knowledge of painting was maintained by those giving expression to religious themes. So, even though the form of expression was limited, the church provided stability, a form, and an interest in the arts and artistic expression which allowed certain skills to be maintained.

Under Charlemagne, we see development in miniature ivory carving and the Carolingian illumination of texts in book form. This again was mainly done by the church.

During the early Renaissance (which began at the end of the Middle Ages and continued up to the beginning of the European religious wars), we find an artistic development divided into two halves—first in the south, and then in the north of Europe.

In the southern Italian Renaissance, mainly centered around Florence and Rome, the period of development was divided into three parts—the early, middle and late Renaissance.

The early Renaissance made great technical advances in design perspective, reawakening an interest in the Roman techniques and adapting them. The middle period took these technical discoveries and rediscoveries further. The late Renaissance polished those techniques and in its final form achieved the perfection one sees in Michelangelo, Raphael and Leonardo da Vinci, to take three examples.

The early Renaissance can first be identified with Cimabue, who (in his few remaining frescoes) advanced anatomical accuracy beyond the Byzantine.

The first person from whom we have more remaining work is Giotto. Philosophically and religiously, these two painters were clearly within the context of a

Christian consensus and tradition, and there is no reason to doubt that they were personally believers as well. So, for instance, we read in Giorgio Vasari's *Lives of the Artists* (in his second edition of 1558, trans. George Bull), when he speaks of Giotto's death: "Eventually in the year 1336, fairly soon after his return from Milan, Giotto, who had made so many beautiful works of art and whose devout life as a Christian matched his achievements as a painter, gave up his soul to God, to the great sorrow of all his fellow citizens and all those who had known him or merely heard his name."

In the second part of the Renaissance, whose era was dominated artistically by Uccello, Ghiberti, Brunelleschi, Donatello, Piero della Francesca, Fra Angelico, Alberti, Fra Filippo Lippi, Botticelli, Verrochio, Mantegna, we find a mixture of clearly Christian painters, painters who held unquestioningly the Christian consensus in general, and a few who were more open to some of the humanistic platonic ideas being introduced at that time by the Medici family and some of their scholars.

Nevertheless, most of these artists were creating within the framework of the church or the church's support, through church commissions, commissions from religious orders, etc. This even includes some of what one would call their "secular" work.

Even for those of the middle Renaissance, who were dabbling with a classical and pagan interest mixed with Christianity (which forms the beginnings of modern humanism, as it has come up to us in our own day), the origin of creativity was placed firmly in God's hands as the Author of all living things, and the general teachings of Scripture were unquestioned.

Some amongst the middle Renaissance painters were most decidedly devout Christians from all we can learn of them. So, for instance, in Vasari's *Lives of the Artists* (once again), we read of Fra Giovanni Angelico, who lived from 1387 to 1455: "Fra Giovanni Angelico of Fiesole, known in the world as 'Guido,' was both an accomplished painter and illuminator, and also a worthy priest, and for the one reason as much as the other should be honored by posterity. He could have lived very prosperously as a layman, satisfying all his material ambitions through the practice of those arts in which he was proficient even when young. But for his own peace and satisfaction and above all for the sake of his soul, being by nature serious and devout, he chose to join the Order of Friars Preachers. For although it is possible to serve God in all walks of life, there are those who believe that they must seek their salvation inside a monastery rather than in the world."

So we see that Vasari, that contemporary historian of the Renaissance, saw no contradiction in terms between one of the great artists of that middle period of the Renaissance being a painter of renown, a Christian, and also a practicing priest. Indeed, at the end of the quote, we even see he makes it quite clear that one could serve God as an artist without being a priest, but that Fra Angelico preferred to remain in the Order. (Naturally, much of Fra Angelico's painting within his Order was of a "religious" nature, since as a priest, he usually was commissioned by his own Order to carry out specific and illustrative tasks.)

In the last period of the Renaissance (after which art technique began to disintegrate into the strange mannerist and the rather pompous, overbearing Baroque period), we see Leonardo da Vinci, Giorgione, Correggio, Raphaël, Michelangelo, and Titian.

The last period of the Renaissance was more humanistic and less religiously oriented. Nevertheless, all was still done very much with the support of the church of the day, and none of the artists mentioned above, even in the last period of the Renaissance, seemed to feel any great contradiction in terms between dividing their work between secular and religious themes.

We even read that Michelangelo, on his deathbed, requested his friends to recall to him the sufferings of Christ. Leonardo, who had explored so much classical pagan thinking in his day, nevertheless called for his confessor, in the presence of the King of France, when dying.

Thus we see even at the high and final period of the Renaissance, which is often considered more humanistic, that Christianity still held a very strong profile, as both a supportive force of the organized church and a personal motivation behind much of the work.

In northern Europe, the historical era following the Renaissance, or rather coinciding with the end of it, was the Reformation, which brought an explosion of creativity.

In the pre-Reformation, the events immediately leading up to the Reformation, we see such figures as

Albrecht Dürer who, devoutly Christian, also had a great understanding of the diversity of God's world. This can be clearly seen when contrasting the massive and apocalyptic themes of Dürer's woodcuts with the time and trouble he takes to portray some of God's smallest creatures in such loving detail, the plants, the flowers, the small rabbit by the wayside.

Artistically, especially in painting, drawing, graphics, and music, the Reformation tradition of northern Europe is unrivaled—a single dazzling contribution to culture and the arts.

The names of Rembrandt and Vermeer are legendary. Theirs was a day and age of confidence, unlike our own wavering times.

For them there was no dichotomy between painting the scene of the common man involved with his trade and the biblical theme. All was God's world, all was redeemed, all was seen as a whole, all came from the hand of God. (Indeed, it was this spirit that led in both Protestant and Catholic Europe to the foundation of early modern science. God's world was perceived as orderly and could be explored.) Spiritual things and the things of the physical world were not given higher or lower status, but all came from God's gracious hand. Thus, with confidence they could march forward and discover this world in science, and celebrate it in the arts.

This was the spirit which produced the great Reformation art. Bach, in his handwriting, put "praise to the Lamb" in the margin of his score; Rembrandt painted his own face as one of those putting Christ on the cross; hundreds of other corroborative facts pointed to the strong Christian involvement on a personal level of so many Reformation men in the arts.

Meanwhile, the arts of the south after the late Renaissance became more and more distant and monumental in nature and had less and less to do with daily life.

By contrast, the art of the Reformation north became more and more human. We see the exquisite painting of light playing on an empty room with only one woman, a housewife, quietly going about her daily chores. The fish seller, the old man by the roadside, these are amongst the subjects of the northern Reformation art. Indeed, they are the subjects of God's world, the subjects of a world which is worthwhile even in its smallest detail, because our Lord has made it. These are the glorious traditions of Western man.

The history of music in the West would be practically and forbiddingly bare without the contributions of Bible-believing Christians, and nonexistent altogether if those who lived within the Christian consensus, unquestioningly accepting its basic premise, were absent.

Ours is the tradition of the great music in which Western man has reveled and gloried for centuries. Again, with no guilty division between the sacred music and the secular, Bach and Handel could write both. Handel wrote *The Messiah*, Handel wrote ballet music. Bach wrote his Cantatas, Bach wrote his Fugues, Bach wrote his hymns, chorals, and even humorous music as in his *Coffee Cantata*. All was seen as part of God's world, all could be done to his glory. One was not higher, sacred, or secular and lower.

Q. You quote from Giorgio Vasari. Who was he and what did he do?

A. Giorgio Vasari was himself a sculptor, architect, and artist of the High Renaissance. He was a competent craftsman, but is best-known for his outstanding and still much loved and read work *The Lives of the Artists*, of which he published two editions. The quotes here are from the second edition. In reading *The Lives of the Artists*, one is struck constantly with his use of terms such as "by the good grace of God," or "God's great gifts to. . . ," and so forth.

Vasari certainly lived in a world in which ultimate meaning was derived from God's own hand and could be measured in moral terms as well as artistic terms.

An expression of inspired confidence based on a sound philosophy, Giorgio Vasari's work makes good reading for anyone who has become sated and sickened by the rather putrid waffling art criticism style of our own day and age. (At one point about thirty years ago certain facts in Vasari's *Lives* were questioned, but, increasingly, modern scholarship is reconfirming much of his accuracy.)

Q. As a Christian in the arts, what style should I be using? What kind of work should I be doing?

A. There is no particularly Christian style. Style is not a question which we must worry about too much. An imposed Christian style becomes stifling and rigid, which leads to redundance in the area of creativity.

Creativity needs freedom. The worth of an art work can be judged in several ways. Judging works of art, that is, the whole body of an artist's work, falls into two categories—first its base and integrity, second the technical style.

The technical style is the less important of the two and is individual with the artist. Technical style can only be judged on the basis of what the artist is obviously trying to accomplish.

Any true discussion of style must be the discussion of the style of a specific artist or group of artists in the context of their actual work, and not merely abstractly as words on paper.

However, in terms of integrity and our philosophical base, here are some thoughts.

The lifelong body of work may truly reflect with integrity (not covering up or with a deluge of propaganda) the whole artist as a whole person, a whole individual, the good, the bad, the discouragements, the good moments, the beauty, the ugliness, the fights, the wrestlings, the quiet, the certitude, the answers, the problems, the love, the compassion, the social statements, the protest, and so on.

Over this lifetime body of work, some only ex-

press a portion of who they are as whole people, some express more, no one perfectly. Nevertheless, there must be a natural outpouring, not a contrived outpouring, and a true manifestation of who that person is as a whole human being, and what his/her interests are. This is why one automatically rejects repetitive propaganda and sloganeering when one realizes how much more there is to any individual, however narrow.

The whole lifetime body of work must progress and not become cliché-ridden or addicted to one easy formula. It must show the integrity of experimentation and the integrity of taking risks, and hopefully at the same time a maturing of one's personal style over the years.

As Christians, the overall lifetime body of work will show something of our lives as based in God himself. This does not necessarily mean implicitly the gospel itself, but what we do choose as subject matter will be ultimately related to our true beliefs, and not in a narrow sloganeering sense.

This is not unique to Christians. Good artists who are non-Christians and have integrity reflect their world views over their lifetime body of works as well. This reflection is not some forced philosphical treatise as an art work, but rather a gradual *natural* outpouring *over the years* of one's personality and one's beliefs, amongst other things.

Beware of those who speak in terms of a right or wrong style, a worldly or an unworldly style. We are stuck in this world. It is not that easy to divide everything up into compartments. The best thing to do as a working individual in the arts is to ignore most people and their advice, which is usually too freely given, and press ahead with one's own work and convictions, realizing that to sit and talk about the arts (including my book) will never replace the act of creating.

Artistic achievement is an individual solo experience most of the time. Even when groups of people combine to make some art work, such as a film, it is a solo experience. We live in an age of collectivism and socialist ideas. These generally destroy the arts, and can be seen to have done so in countries where the arts are regarded purely as socialist propaganda. Resist these collective pressures. An individual is unique; the sum total of a group is nothing.

There is not a right or wrong amount of philosophic expression in an art work. I, for instance, have painted many paintings which have no direct philosophical content in the narrow sense. On the other hand, I have made films that have a direct philosophical and social content mirroring my own beliefs, while other parts of those same films have been more purely artistic.

It is the lifetime body of work, I repeat, which stacks up. You do not say everything in one art work, nor should you try. The amount of active philosophizing and social activity that goes on in art is purely up to the individual and does not make the work of art higher or lower. To each his own.

As far as style goes, there is no modern style. An art work is modern if it has been made recently, that is the end of it. The style mirrors the individual artist as much as the content does. Style should remain individual and at the same time not be so self-conscious that it seeks to be individual for individuality's sake. We can and should learn from and enjoy others' work.

The old apprenticeship system in painting was not such a bad one. Rudiments and useful tools were learned in a strict atmosphere from which then gradually the artist would drift away and develop as he later matured.

At the same time, in the apprenticeship system artists were able to contribute to real finished works of art rather than just experiments, and the graduation of an artist was not something that happened overnight with a diploma, but was gradually moved into.

(Interestingly enough, this system exists in several fields still. Cinema is one of them, where there is a gradual progression of working from simpler to harder films or from simpler to harder jobs within the film industry.)

As regards style in any area, we can always enjoy and learn from the style of others, realizing that all style is a progression of the whole human family. Copy or not copy as we wish, we have great freedom.

Some styles present passing short-term problems with having been heavily identified with specifically anti-Christian statements. However, these specifically anti-Christian statements are few and far betwen, compared to the whole artistic flow of mankind, which is usually too busy doing too many other things. Again there must be freedom in choosing styles. We cannot bind other people in this area.

Lastly in this note, there is the question of performing art works (as musicians, dancers, or opera singers for instance) of other artists, or as commercial artists or as artists creating a work on commission.

Again I would say there is tremendous freedom here. *The main point is that you are actively practicing the talent which God has given you.* What you perform or do not perform, make or not make is not the point. The point is that you are living out who you are as a person made in God's image.

A rare question will arise of Christians performing or not performing in specifically anti-Christian plays, for instance. Again, these decisions must be made by the individual with integrity and courage, and based on one situation at a time in which he or she finds himself or herself. The same is true in the choice of clients or subjects in the commercial art field.

This decision is no more or less complicated than others we make through our relationship with the world in general—for instance, we decide whether or not to pay taxes to a government which, for example, actively supports a national health system which gives free abortions, or the government of the United States which actively supports organizations such as Planned Parenthood which act as antifamily, propromiscuous, proabortion forces within our society.

Christian artists must not allow themselves to be forced into making tougher choices than the general Christian public is willing to make. It must cut both ways. At the same time, artists should show courage and, when needed, go down fighting for artistic integrity on the one hand and against the humanistic pagan culture on the other hand.

Q. As someone in the arts and the field of communication, what specifically should I be doing now?

A. Real creative talent manifests itself only in one way:
work accomplished. True creativity does not ask, "What
shall I do? What can I do?" The truly creative person
who excels in his or her field has a driving conviction
that *forces* high productivity almost by instinct.

Those who sit around and talk the arts are rarely
creating artistic works. Like most critics, they are better
at theorizing than at producing.

Real artistic discussion is not theorizing, and it
usually occurs between working partners or friends as
they consider concrete, physical, actual problems of
ongoing work, including the battle against secular hu-
manist dominance of communications.

Q. As a Christian in the arts, should I work in the
secular world or Christian world?

A. Let me answer, once and for all, there is *no* secular
or Christian world. There is only one world, the whole
world as God has made it. This is common scientific
knowledge acquired usually by the first grade. It is only
the Christian thinkers who have, unfortunately, not
noticed this fact. The terms "secular" and "Christian"
are only words. Reality cannot be compartmentalized.
If we Christians have lost our influence in some part of
the world's activities we must reclaim it.

Q. How could I possibly find time for all of these things?

A. First and most basic—turn off the television. Rethink your time. Many activities of life are of no real lasting value. Reduce your church activities. Remember, *the whole world is God's world.* Explaining this concept to children at an art museum will be far more effective than abstract talk at Sunday school.

Read with discernment. Forget "how-to" books that provide shortcuts to God. The classics (and many modern books) contain the gamut of human experience.

This may sound like a lot of work, but remember, as you involve yourself, enjoyment and satisfaction will be the result. Unlike an intensive lifelong study of a dry theology, creativity and art come under the pleasurable category of entertainment, as well as having other deep qualities.

Q. As a parent, what are you doing to encourage your own children in these areas?

A. No TV, at least on any level that can be called regular watching. Genie and I read works we consider to be of pleasurable literary value to them out loud each evening (easy to find—the English language is rich in children's literature). We try to bring them up to higher standards instead of talking down to them (as television thrives upon doing). We try to present as wide a panorama of culture exposure as is possible, and express something of the diverse beauty of God's world and his creatures' creations.

We watch films together as a family and talk about them later, a great pleasure and a way to understand the world.

We read long portions of the Bible together (not a children's paraphrase of Bible stories, but a good modern translation—NIV). They come to a deeper understanding of God's world this way.

We try to offer honest answers to their questions, including "I don't know" when we don't. In reading the Bible to them, we don't skip the awkward parts. By the time a child has had Genesis, Exodus, First and Second Samuel read to him, there is nothing he doesn't know about!

We do careful work on home environment: décor, music, food, plants, pointing out beauty wherever possible.

We teach them that compassion comes from a high view of individual worth. We do not practice an uptight filtering out of all modern culture to avoid embarrassing or difficult questions.

We teach them that the whole world is God's. Playing with them as children and talking with them as seriously as we would with any adult: these things will help to give them an appreciation of art, life, quality, standards, people, themselves, God. We avoid pietistic "Christian activities," and "Christian children's stories," etc., as if that was what Christianity was all about. We pickett abortion clinics together. Real life and Christianity must be one, not separate compartments. The world is where we live, not the church. And again nature, beauty, nature, nature, and nature!

Children in Christian homes must grow up understanding the problems they will face as adults; they must learn to be ready to fight for Christian values, and not be timid, complacent "good citizens." They must also learn to enjoy the beauty God has given us in *this* life now.

Q. How can I better acquaint myself with the many areas of human creative involvement of which you speak?

A. An enjoyment and appreciation of the arts hinges upon your willingness to absorb and reflect upon the artistic endeavors of others. No one who has not partaken, on a regular basis, of the rich heritage of those who have gone before, or of our own talented contemporaries, can truly be acquainted with or appreciate the human species as a creative creature. This enjoyment of others is as essential to understanding and developing our *own* creative ability as the work we do ourselves.

The museums and galleries of the world cry out for inspection. North America as well as Europe contain a wealth of diversity in exhibitions, movies, retrospectives, music festivals, touring dance companies, opera, theatre (from local productions to Broadway casts), orchestras. To ignore these in total is sad indeed.

Enjoyment of the vast diversity of music is easily available today through the high technology of stereo recording. Concerts, individual performances, recordings of music spanning the entire written history of the human race are at our fingertips. Subscribe to concert series, attend recitals, take architectural tours. Almost every region of the world is a ferment of creative and cultural activity; the possiblities are as diverse as God's creatures.

Take an active interest in those individuals exhibiting creative potential around you. Encourage them. Do they paint? Buy one of their works. Do they play a musical instrument? Arrange for them to perform for others. Do they write? Help them publish. Do they compose? Listen. Do they make films? Invest in a film production. Are they in politics? Vote for them.

To be unaware or unappreciative of art in its broadest scope is to border on mulish stupidity. The sheer diversity of what is available that is excellent makes even more pathetic those who turn to mediocrity.

Q. What can people who are not in the arts themselves, but interested in a more creative and sensitive existence, do to improve their awareness about the matters you have been talking about?

A. First, we must realize that our environment, what we surround ourselves with, look at, enjoy, absorb, consciously or unconsciously, all affects us far more than we think. Therefore, it is of the utmost importance to realize that our home, the materials it is made of, decorated with, what we read, look at, enjoy, where we worship, entertainment, etc. all add up to a great force in our life for good or evil, depending on what we have chosen.

Home environment, decoration, what you watch or do not watch on TV (if any), magazines, the newspaper, books we read, etc.—all must be chosen with great care indeed. When we watch something or read something, we should discuss it. If you do not have time to discuss and analyze what you are reading, watching, looking at, observing, then you do not have time to watch it. For me, that is a rule. No time to discuss, then no time to watch.

Many people, through a lack of understanding of the importance of their environment, allow themselves to be partially handicapped by what they look at. For some, it will be a long hard road to undo the damage of the thick calloused insensitivity developed inside themselves from unthinkingly watching any and all things on television, or by never questioning the aesthetic effects of the various materials used to build or to decorate their home (e.g., surrounding themselves with plastic imitations instead of natural things, and allowing the worst of Christian art to infiltrate their homes in the form of magazines, books, pictures on their walls, TV and so forth). All this can add up to a terrible handicap in terms of seeing real beauty, worth, integrity, and in developing a true sense of quality in one's personal taste. An active effort must be made to roll back time in order to be able to discern and nurture an appreciation of quality in each area. Since so much of the output of the church is poor, we should be especially careful to keep it away from us. Don't let your images and ideas about God himself and truth be polluted by mediocre teaching, magazines, books, radio, and TV. Christian rubbish is the most destructive of all. Keep away from it, stop your ears, cover your eyes.

Here, there is no time to go into further detail, except to say that the main point, once again, is your environment. What you watch, what you absorb mentally *does* contribute to who you are as a person, your understanding of the world around you, of other people, and of God. It is important. What you surround yourself with will either enrich your life, or impoverish you. It will either bring you closer to God's whole world, other people, beauty, and aesthetic enjoyment, or put a barrier between you and these things. The main point is this: take what you surround yourself with seriously, take what you watch seriously. You can't breathe poisonous air and get away with it. Similarly, do not think you can get away with living in a shoddy environment, dedicated to mediocrity, even if the ingredients come marked "Christian."

Q. Do you have suggestions for some further reading to do on the subject you have been discussing?

A. The following is a short list:

> *Four Arguments for the Elimination of Television,* Jerry Mander (New York: Morrow, 1978)

I highly recommend this book by Jerry Mander as *the* definitive text on the problems of television, particularly in the United States. It points out clearly a serious problem with television as a technology itself, its content, its limitations, and what it does to people. The book covers secular TV, but all it says is equally true of the present rash of Christian TV.

> *Panic Among the Philistines,* Bryan Griffin (Chicago: Regnery-Gateway, 1983)

This wonderful book is the best exposé of the bankruptcy of Western modern art and literature. It is a funny and well-written discussion of Western culture of the twentieth century without God.

> *Art and the Bible,* Francis A. Schaeffer (Downers Grove, Ill.: InterVarsity Press, 1973)

Art and the Bible is a good corroborative statement of this volume in detailing the uses of art and creativity within the Bible itself, particularly in such areas as the Tabernacle. It can easily be read at a sitting and is an excellent follow-up to this volume.

> *Modern Art and the Death of a Culture,* H. R. Rookmaaker (Downers Grove, Ill.: InterVaristy Press, 1970)

While not on the specific subjects covered in this volume, Dr. Rookmaaker's book is of tremendous importance in understanding the historical and philosphical background against which the artist today must work.

> *The Creative Gift: Essays on Art and the Christian Life*, H. R. Rookmaaker (Westchester, Ill.: Crossway Books, 1980)

This later book by Rookmaaker, published posthumously, deals directly with many of the issues facing Christians in the arts today. It is especially helpful in showing how our calling as creatures who are created in the image of God relates to creativity, artistic freedom, and communicating the Gospel in the modern world.

> *How Should We Then Live?* Francis A. Schaeffer (Westchester, Ill.: Crossway Books, 1983. Film series distributed by Gospel Films Inc., Muskegon, Michigan)

To understand the church today and the dilemma facing Christians in our day and age, we must understand not only the twentieth century, but where it came from.

How Should We Then Live? is the master text dealing with the relationship between Christians and history, their contribution and the opposing philosophical system which has hounded Christians for hundreds of years (that is, a humanistic thought form).

For anyone who actually wants to do something in this day and age, this is mandatory reading. For those involved in the arts and cultural endeavors, *How Should We Then Live?* looks carefully and closely at these subjects in our recent times and more distant past.

It traces Western man's development from the time of the collapse of the Roman Empire up into our own day, and the authoritarian governmental systems that we face. A challenge, a warning. See the films also.

> *Artists of the Renaissance*, Giorgio Vasari (Selection from *Lives of the Artists*, trans. George Bull, London: Alan Lane, Penguin Books)

For those who do not have time to study the full *Lives of the Artists*, this selection of the principal artists' lives and the introductions is invaluable.

> *Has Modernism Failed?*, Suzi Gablik (New York: Thames Hudson, 1984)

This book is the last word for the serious art history student on the plight of Western culture in the post-Christian era. A must for any professional artist in this generation.

> *The Life of Giorgio Vasari*, Robert W. Cardon (London: Lee Warner, 1910)

A book for those who have an interest in Giorgio Vasari, and having read his *Lives of the Artists*, wish to read something about him.

> *The Spirit of Enterprise*, George Gilder (New York: Simon & Schuster, 1984)

A good book to illustrate the way in which creativity applies to *all* areas of life, including business and commerce. Everyone can and should be creative. Society functions because of its most imaginative citizens, teaches Gilder.

> *No Other Foundation*, Jeremy Jackson (Westchester, Ill.: Crossway, 1979)

For those with an interest in the roots and origins of Christianity and the sources of the present modern-day dilemmas and weaknesses facing the church, Jackson's book is invaluable, stimulating, and well written. Written by a true scholar in every sense of the word, who (unlike most scholars) clearly communicates his ideas, and applies them to real issues, rather than playing with footnotes.

> *The Origins of Christian Art*, Michael Gough (London: Thames and Hudson, 1973)

This is a volume which covers the first eight centuries of Christian art. It is interesting because it serves to illustrate the richness and the diversity of Christians' involvements in the arts in the earliest centuries of the church.

> *Whatever Happened to the Human Race?* Francis A. Schaeffer/C. Everett Koop (Westchester, Ill.: Crossway Books, 1983. Film series Franky Schaeffer V Productions Inc., Los Gatos, Calif.)

A good example of another area neglected by a pietistic, silent church. Real action on behalf of individuals, not conveniently on the other side of the world, but right here on our doorstep.

This book deals with the biblical Christian response to the monstrous idea that there is such a thing as a life not worthy to be lived. Abortion, infanticide and euthanasia are the key examples. Schaeffer and Koop call for a stand against these evils.

This book fits in very well with the concepts herein, as a study on utilitarianism carried to its logical conclusion, and as a call to Christians to involve themselves with the whole of life. See the films also.

And lastly, the wealth of the centuries of English literature, wit, and wisdom that is our heritage, and which until the very recent past was dominated by Christian thinking.

ABOUT THE AUTHOR

Franky Schaeffer V was born in Switzerland. His parents, Dr. Francis and Edith Schaeffer, founded the international study and religious community, L'Abri Fellowship.

The beginning of Franky Schaeffer's professional life vis-à-vis the arts and creativity was in his painting, graphics (principally woodcuts), drawing and sculpture. Franky Schaeffer as a painter has had a number of successful one-man shows in various countries. Among these were a show at the Frisch Gallery in New York, Chante-Pierre Gallery in Aubonne, Switzerland (near Geneva), and several showings courtesy of Criteria Arts and Mr. and Mrs. Bazlington in London. In addition to these, he had numberous paintings and drawings hanging and selling from other galleries in the United States and Europe. He supported his family for five years as a painter in Switzerland.

Throughout the time he was painting, he experimented in still photography and film.

An opportunity to do something more serious in film arose when he conceived the idea of producing a series which was released under the title *How Should We Then Live?* This featured his father as writer and narrator and was produced by Franky Schaeffer. He worked two and a half years on this project.

Following the successful conclusion and release of this series, Franky Schaeffer, with Jim Buchfuehrer, formed a nonprofit film and media company, Franky Schaeffer V Productions. Since its formation, Franky Schaeffer has written and directed the well-known five-hour film series *Whatever Happened to the Human Race?* The making of this series was a two-year endeavor. Since that time he has written and directed the films *Reclaiming the World* and *The Second American Revolution,* and co-written and produced the film *The Great Evangelical Disaster.* He has also written three additional books: *A Time for Anger, Bad News for Modern Man,* and *A Modest Proposal.*

Franky Schaeffer has spoken to many audiences in the United States and abroad on the topic of this book. At present he is working on several new film projects of his own. In addition, he is involved in various publishing projects and is the literary agent for Edith Schaeffer, C. Everett Koop, M.D., John Whitehead and other authors.

Franky Schaeffer edits *The Christian Activist* newspaper, a free quarterly published by Schaeffer Productions. He and his wife are the parents of three children.

ABOUT THE ILLUSTRATOR

Kurt Mitchell studied fine art at Millikin University where he received a BFA in studio drawing and painting. Twice cited for excellence by the Evangelical Press Association, he has illustrated numerous covers and articles for InterVarsity Press, *His* magazine, *Christianity Today,* and the *Chicago Tribune.* Since 1979 he has divided his time between illustrating and designing animation for the Cioni Artworks. He currently works and resides in Chicago.

LIST OF ILLUSTRATIONS